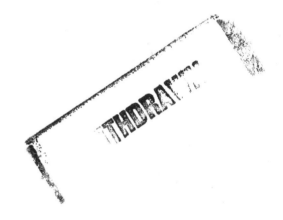

LIGHTNING
BOLT
BOOKS™

Endangered and Extinct Invertebrates

Jennifer Boothroyd

Lerner Publications Company
Minneapolis

For my friend
Nathan W.
–J.B.

Lerner Publications Company
A division of Lerner Publishing Group, Inc.
241 First Avenue North
Minneapolis, MN 55401 U.S.A.

For reading levels and more information, look up this title at www.lernerbooks.com.

Library of Congress Cataloging-in-Publication Data

Boothroyd, Jennifer, 1972–
    Endangered and extinct invertebrates / by Jennifer Boothroyd.
        pages cm. — (Lightning bolt books. Animals in danger)
    Includes index.
    ISBN 978-1-4677-1333-7 (lib. bdg. : alk. paper)
    ISBN 978-1-4677-2495-1 (eBook)
        1. Rare invertebrates—Juvenile literature. 2. Extinct invertebrates—Juvenile literature. I. Title.
    QL362.45.B66 2014
    592.168—dc23   2013020700

Manufactured in the United States of America
1 — PC — 12/31/13

Table of Contents

invertebrates

Invertebrates are animals without backbones. There are many types of invertebrates.

These animals are invertebrates.

Some invertebrates are in trouble. They are endangered. Endangered animals are in danger of dying out.

The Delta green ground beetle is endangered.

Endangered Invertebrates

Greek red
damsels
are bright
red.

This insect is
also endangered.

The damsels live by streams.
They eat small insects.

Polluted waters are dangerous for Greek red damsels.

What's sitting on that leaf?
It's an Oahu tree snail. It lives in a mountain forest.

Not many Oahu tree snails are left.

The snails are small. Their shells have different colors.

This scientist is releasing an endangered snail into its natural environment.

Tiny algae live on coral. The coral gets its food from the algae.

Staghorn coral lives in the ocean. The coral is endangered.

Water that is too warm or too cold can harm the coral.

This coral is not healthy.

The pink velvet worm has fuzzy skin.

Pink velvet worms live under dead leaves in a forest similar to this one.

The worms live in Weza-Ngele Forest in South Africa. Their habitat is getting smaller.

People built roads and cut down trees. The worms are in trouble.

White-clawed crayfish live in streams.

This crayfish's claws are white underneath.

They are found in Europe.

The crayfish hide under rocks and tree roots. They eat small fish and insects.

The white-clawed crayfish population is shrinking. These people are working on a project to help save them.

Extinct Invertebrates

Meganeura are extinct. They have completely died out.

These insects lived millions of years ago.

This dragonfly was huge.
Some had wingspans over
2 feet (61 centimeters) long.

Trilobites lived in the ocean.
They had hard outer shells.

Trilobites died out 240 million years ago.

People learn about trilobites from fossils. Fossils are hardened remains of animals or plants.

There were twenty thousand kinds of trilobites. Here are just a few.

Ammonites lived deep in the ocean. They went extinct 65 million years ago.

This animal's shell protected its soft body.

The largest of these animals were 9 feet (3 meters) across.

Some ammonites were small. Others were very big.

Aldabra banded snails
had striped shells.
The last snail was
found in 1997.

Aldabra banded snails were once easy to find on the Aldabra Islands near Africa.

The land where the snails lived dried up. Not enough rain fell. The snails died off.

Scientists ask questions and do experiments to discover things like why certain animals go extinct.

Arcuate pearly mussels lived in the United States. They are extinct.

Mussels have soft bodies inside hard shells. This is a Higgins eye pearly mussel.

These mussels lived in rivers.
They ate algae.

Arcuate pearly mussels have not been seen since 2000.

Helping Endangered Invertebrates

Many people try to help endangered invertebrates. They remove invasive plants. These are plants that can harm other plants and animals in an area.

People also clean up the land where endangered invertebrates live. Clean land helps invertebrates survive.

These people help by picking up trash.

What You Can Do

There are many things you can do to help endangered invertebrates.

- Clean up trash from land and water.

- Walk, bike, or ride the bus instead of using a car.

- Remove invasive plants.

- Learn about climate change.

- Recycle things to create less trash.

- Don't use chemicals on your lawn or garden.

- Support zoos and other animal organizations.

A Remarkable Recovery

The ladybird spider lives in England. There were fewer than fifty of these spiders in 1993. Too many invasive plants were in their habitat. Many people helped remove the plants. The spider's habitat grew healthier. More than one thousand ladybird spiders were found in 2008!

Glossary

algae: tiny plants without roots

climate: Earth's weather conditions over a long period of time. When these conditions change, plants and animals may be affected.

endangered: at risk of dying out

extinct: died out

fossil: the hardened remains of an animal or plant

habitat: where an animal lives

invasive: a word to describe plants and animals that enter a habitat and cause unwanted changes

invertebrate: an animal without a backbone

population: the number of living members of a group

Further Reading

Dell'Oro, Suzanne Paul.
Let's Look at Earthworms.
Minneapolis: Lerner Publications, 2011.

Dialogue for Kids: Endangered Species
http://idahoptv.org/dialogue4kids/season9
/endspecies/facts.cfm

Hoare, Ben, and Tom Jackson. Endangered
Animals. New York: DK Publishing, 2010.

National Geographic Kids: Green Invaders
http://kids.nationalgeographic.com/kids/stories
/spacescience/invasive-plants

San Diego Zoo
http://kids.sandiegozoo.org/animals/insects

Silverman, Buffy. Do You Know about Insects?
Minneapolis: Lerner Publications, 2010.

World Wildlife Federation: Go Wild
http://gowild.wwf.org.uk

Index

Photo Acknowledgments

The images in this book are used with the permission of: © Joel Sartore/National Geographic/Getty Images, pp. 2, 24; © Verastuchelova/Dreamstime.com, p. 4 (top left); © EcoPrint/Shutterstock.com, p. 4 (top right); © iStockphoto.com/GlobalP, p. 4 (bottom left); © Wayne Mckown/Dreamstime.com, p. 4 (bottom right); Aneedtoknow/Wikimedia Commons, p. 5; © Johannes van Donge - www.Diginature.nl, p. 6; Joe Blossom/Balance/Photoshot./Newscom, p. 7; © Nathan Yuen, p. 8; U.S. Air Force photo/Tech Sgt Michael R. Holzworth, p. 9; Amanda Meyer/U.S. Fish and Wildlife Service, p. 10; © Reinhard Dirscherl/WaterFrame/Getty Images, p. 11; © Peter Chadwick/Science Source, p. 12; © Rodger Shagam/Gallo Images/Getty Images, p. 13; © Wolfgang Poelzer/WaterFrame/Getty Images, p. 14; © Linda Pitkin/2020VISION/naturepl.com, p. 15; © www.surfacevision.com, p. 16; © Walter Myers/Science Source, pp. 17, 18; © Cristina Arias/Cover/Getty Images, p. 19; © Paul Fleet/Shutterstock.com, p. 20; © Biophoto Associates/Science Source, p. 21; © Martin Harvey/Gallo Images/Getty Images, p. 22; © Thomas Tolstrup/Riser/Getty Images, p. 23; © John R. Kreul/Independent Picture Service, p. 25; © Jim West/age fotostock/SuperStock, p. 26; © AE Pictures Inc./Photodisc/Getty Images, p. 27; © blickwinkel/Alamy, p. 29; © Brenden Holland, PhD, Pacific Biosciences Research Center, University of Hawaii, p. 30.

Front Cover: © Photo by Brett Cortesi, courtesy of Roger Williams Park Zoo www.rwpzoo.org (bottom); © Paul Fleet/Shutterstock.com (top).

Main body text set in Johann Light 30/36.